1st Workshop on Explainable Computational Intelligence (XCI 2017)

Santiago de Compostela, Spain
4 September 2017

ISBN: 978-1-5108-4859-7

Printed from e-media with permission by:

Curran Associates, Inc.
57 Morehouse Lane
Red Hook, NY 12571

Some format issues inherent in the e-media version may also appear in this print version.

Printed by Curran Associates, Inc. (2017)

For permission requests, please contact the Association for Computational Linguistics at the address below.

Association for Computational Linguistics
209 N. Eighth Street
Stroudsburg, Pennsylvania 18360

Phone: 1-570-476-8006
Fax: 1-570-476-0860

acl@aclweb.org

Additional copies of this publication are available from:

Curran Associates, Inc.
57 Morehouse Lane
Red Hook, NY 12571 USA
Phone: 845-758-0400
Fax: 845-758-2633
Email: curran@proceedings.com
Web: www.proceedings.com

INLG 2017

Proceedings of the 1st Workshop on Explainable Computational Intelligence

XCI 2017

September 4, 2017
Santiago de Compostela, Spain

Preface

In recent years, a torrent of Computational Intelligence (CI) applications with an outstanding autonomous degree in their behaviour has been successfully developed (e.g., fuzzy controllers, neural networks, genetic algorithms, etc). These systems can operate without human intervention and achieve unbeatable results; however, at the same time and as a result of this success, their complexity has been dramatically increased. Thus, for the typical user, these systems become *black boxes* and he or she has to blindly trust in them.

Given this context, the problem of **explainability** arises. Its main goal can be described as transforming these *black-box* systems into *glass-box* ones, where the end user can understand the reasons that support the system's decisions. For instance, when an expert system in medicine advises a patient to take a particular drug for treating his disease, he or she needs to know why these are the right drugs for his or her disease.

During the last two years several workshops has been organised around the topic of explainability in computational systems, mainly in Artificial Intelligence (known as Explainable Artificial Intelligence - XAI). Mostly of them have been focused on machine learning, one of the current hot topics in AI, and how these techniques can produce more *explainable models*. In the case of CI, this issue is already in its agenda from some time ago and has been addressed by the studies in *interpretability*, which main goal is to keep the inner structure of the CI systems as clear as possible both for engineers and users. Thus, for that reason, in the Workshop on Explainable Computational Intelligence (XCI), we focus on other two challenges typical in explainability studies: *explanation interface* and *psychology of explanation*.

Explanation interface is directly related with the techniques to generate effective explanations for human users. Therefore, the use of **natural language**, as the main tool for human communication, perfectly suits to this aim. Holding the XCI during the International Natural Language Generation (INLG) brings us the chance of tackling this hurdle from a multidisciplinary perspective and put the grounds for a new collaboration space between both communities.

Psychology of explanation points out, precisely, to the necessity of a computational theory of explanation. Currently, there is a gap between the **machine logic**, which underlies this type of systems, and **human logic** and, consequently, building a bridge between them is a necessary step to make them more explainable and understandable. In CI, a computational theory of perceptions has been developed and successfully applied, and, for that reason, the experience gathered by the researchers in this field will provide some relevant clues for the development of the aforementioned computational theory of explanation.

In this first edition of the XCI, we have received seven submissions of short papers and four of them appear in this volume. In addition, we have an invited talk by Dr. Jose M. Alsonso (University of Santiago de Compostela), who has a broad experience in the topic of interpretability in CI systems.

We would like to thank the Program Committee members who reviewed the papers and helped to improve the overall quality of the workshop. We also thank the General Chairs and Workshop Chairs of INLG Conference the given us the chance to organise this workshop. Last, a word of thanks goes to our invited speaker, Dr. Jose M. Alonso.

August 31, 2017
Dundee (Scotland)

Martín Pereira-Fariña
Chris Reed
Co-Organizers of XCI 2017

Organizers:

Martin Pereira-Fariña	University of Dundee & University of Santiago de Compostela
Chris Reed	University of Dundee & Polish Academy of Sciences

Program Committee:

João Paulo Carvalho	Instituto Superior Tecnico / INESC-ID
Pablo Gamallo	University of Santiago de Compostela
Albert Gatt	University of Malta
Lluis Godo	Artificial Intelligence Research Institute, IIIA - CSIC
Floriana Grasso	University of Liverpool
Helmut Horacek	Saarland University
Martín Pereira-Fariña	University of Santiago de Compostela
Chris Reed	University of Dundee
Patrick Saint-Dizier	IRIT-CNRS
Alejandro Sobrino	University of Santiago de Compostela
Adam Wyner	University of Aberdeen

Invited Speaker:

Jose M. Alonso	University of Santiago de Compostela

Table of Contents

Two Challenges for CI Trustworthiness and How to Address Them
Kevin Baum, Maximilian A. Köhl and Eva Schmidt 1

A Simple Method for Clarifying Sentences with Coordination Ambiguities
Michael White, Manjuan Duan and David L. King 6

Requirements for Conceptual Representations of Explanations and How Reasoning Systems Can Serve Them
Helmut Horacek 11

An Essay on Self-explanatory Computational Intelligence: A Linguistic Model of Data Processing Systems
Jose M. Alonso and Gracian Trivino 16

Workshop Program

08:30 - 09:30 **Registration**

09:00 - 09:10 **Presentation**

09:10 - 10:10 **Invited talk by Jose M. Alonso (University of Santiago de Compostela)**

10:10 - 11:00 **Logic and explanation in XCI and NLG**

- **10:10 - 10:35** *Two Challenges for CI Trustworthiness and How to Address Them*
  Kevin Baum, Maximilian A. Köhl and Eva Schmidt

- **10:35 - 11:00** *A Simple Method for Clarifying Sentences with Coordination Ambiguities*
  Michael White, Manjuan Duan and David L. King

11:00 - 11:30 **Coffee Break**

11:30 - 12:20 **Session 2: Challenges in XCI and NLG**

- **11:30 - 11:55** *Requirements for Conceptual Representations of Explanations and How Reasoning Systems Can Serve Them*
  Helmut Horacek

- **11:55 - 12:20** *An Essay on Self-explanatory Computational Intelligence: A Linguistic Model of Data Processing Systems*
  Jose M. Alonso and Gracian Trivino

12:20 - 13:20 **Open discussion and future plans**

13:20 - 13:30 **Wrap-up**

Invited talk

eXplainable Computational Intelligence: paving the way from Smart to Cognitive Cities

Jose M. Alonso
josemaria.alonso.moral@usc.es

Centro de Investigación en Tecnoloxías da Informacíon (CiTIUS)
Universidade de Santiago de Compostela

Abstract

In the era of the Internet of Things, there has been a huge effort connecting all kind of devices to Internet.

Accordingly, in modern cities, everything is connected to Internet. Thus, human beings face two main challenges:

- to extract valuable knowledge from the given Big Data (Data Scientists are more and more demanded by companies);
- to become part of the equation, i.e., to become active actors in the Internet of Things (in our daily life).

Researchers and developers have already created more and more intelligent devices which populate the so-called smart cities.

Moreover, nowadays the focus is set on knowledge representation and how to enhance human-machine interaction, i.e., it is time to address the effective interaction between intelligent systems and citizens with the aim of passing from Smart to Cognitive Cities. Non-expert users, i.e., users without a strong background on Artificial Intelligence (AI), require a new generation of eXplainable AI (XAI) systems. They are expected to naturally interact with humans, thus providing comprehensible explanations of decisions automatically made. In this talk, we sketch how certain Computational Intelligence (CI) techniques, namely interpretable fuzzy systems, are ready to play a key role in the development of XCI systems, i.e., CI-based XAI systems.

Two Challenges for CI Trustworthiness and How to Address Them

Kevin Baum and **Maximilian A. Köhl** and **Eva Schmidt**
Saarland University, Department of Philosophy
k.baum@mx.uni-saarland.de and mail@koehlma.de and eva.schmidt@mx.uni-saarland.de

Abstract

We argue that, to be trustworthy, Computational Intelligence (CI) has to do what it is entrusted to do for permissible reasons and to be able to give rationalizing explanations of its behavior which are accurate and graspable. We support this claim by drawing parallels with trustworthy human persons, and we show what difference this makes in a hypothetical CI hiring system. Finally, we point out two challenges for trustworthy CI and sketch a mechanism which could be used to generate sufficiently accurate as well as graspable rationalizing explanations for CI behavior.

1 Trustworthiness in Humans

For a human person to be trustworthy, she not only has to be competent at the action or decision we trust her with, but also to be appropriately motivated so to act or to decide (McLeod, 2015). To take an example from Kant (1997), the honest merchant who never cheats his customers because he worries about his reputation is someone his customers can *rely* on to be honest. He isn't trustworthy, however, for he is motivated by self-interest, not by goodwill or moral considerations. The trustworthy person is someone who has a disposition to act in a way that warrants our trust in her, for she does what we entrusted her to do for the right reasons.

Importantly, to maintain another's reasonable trust, a person has to be able to explain the motives of her actions. Imagine that you break a promise to help your friend move. This might cause her to stop trusting you—but you may avoid this result if you explain to her that you were committed to helping, but that you had to take your father to the hospital. Note that this explanation only adds to your trust*worthiness* if it is not a made-up excuse, but an *accurate* account of why you didn't do as promised, i.e., an account of your actual reasons.

2 Lessons for Trustworthy CI

These considerations make the following operationalization plausible: A CI system is fully trustworthy if and only if it (1) generally does competently what it is entrusted to do, (2) it does so for permissible reasons, (3) it is able to explain its actions[1] by reference to the reasons for which it acted, and (4) its explanations are accurate. Here, we will focus on conditions (2) to (4).

2.1 Rationalizing Explanations

What kind of explanation is sufficient to make trusting a CI system reasonable? To support our claims that we need explanations that appeal to *reasons* for which the system acted as it did (or rationalizing explanations), take the example of an automated hiring system used by a bank. Imagine that it ranks a young black woman at the bottom of the list of applicants. What would it take for her to reasonably trust that the system's decision was fair?

Clearly, an explanation in terms of a subsymbolic execution protocol[2] leading up to the decision—though it may be a true causal explanation—is

[1] Decisions are included under actions in this paper.

[2] Depending on the implementation of the subsymbolic CI system, we can obtain protocols of different forms. For instance, for a neural network we can obtain a protocol in terms of a description of all neurons and a trace of all signals.

Proceedings of the 1st Workshop on Explainable Computational Intelligence, pages 1–5, Santiago de Compostela, Spain, September 4 2017.

beside the point, for it can't help her determine whether the decision was fair/morally permissible. Rather, what is needed is a rationalizing explanation of the system's decision (Davidson, 1963), which makes the decision rationally intelligible. Rationalizing explanations appeal to the *goals* that the system pursues—sorting the applicants in order of qualification—and the *information* that it used to determine how to achieve its goals—e.g. the applicants' prior work experience. Taken together, explanations that appeal to the system's goals and information, i.e., to the reasons for which it acted, may increase its trustworthiness. In the example, if the system's explanation of its decision includes the information that the young black woman lacked the requisite work experience, she will be able to understand what motivated it and that its decision was indeed permissible.

2.2 Accurate and Permissible Explanations

Moreover, CI systems need to give *accurate* rationalizing explanations to be trustworthy. A system that gives an 'explanation' distinct from what actually drove its decision is not deserving of our trust.

Imagine that the automated hiring system excluded the young black woman not because she lacked relevant work experience, but because it is biased against people of color (Caliskan et al., 2017). If the system explains its decision by giving reasons that were causally irrelevant to the decision but make it appear permissible, there is a reason for the applicant to *reduce* her trust in it. By contrast, if an accurate explanation of what led up to its decision is provided in terms of its mistaken informational state that people of color are less qualified for the job (its bias), this will have less negative impact on the machine's trustworthiness. If we can trust that a system accurately explains its actions, we have no reason to believe that it is 'covering up' its impermissible decisions or actions.[3]

So, accurate rationalizing explanations may be given for actions that are impermissible and still make them intelligible to the persons affected. That there were certain reasons for which the system acted doesn't mean these were *good* reasons. Whether a CI system's action is permissible hinges on whether the reasons for which it was performed were permissible. To determine whether the action was permissible or not, a person then needs an accurate explanation of what motivated it.

We can distinguish *moral* (im)permissibility from *practical* (im)permissibility. A reason for which a CI system acted is morally permissible just in case it violates no moral requirements. It is practically permissible to the extent that actions motivated by it contribute to achieving what the CI system was designed to achieve.

2.3 Graspable Explanations

Further, we need CI systems to give explanations we can grasp. Assume that a system has identified a property which makes an applicant who has it the perfect employee. Its concept of the property—call it 'blagh'—is beyond our understanding. The CI system might accurately rationalize its decision by pointing out that the top applicant has *blagh*. Unfortunately, even so, we are unable to understand it, as we do not possess the concept *blagh*.[4]

2.4 Three Dimensions of Explanations

Following the insights from 2.1, 2.2 and 2.3, we can, aside from the *kind* of an explanation—merely causal vs. rationalizing—, identify the following dimensions of an explanation:

Accuracy: An explanation of an action is accurate if and only if it appeals to what actually led to the action. A rationalizing explanation is accurate if and only if it appeals to the goals and information that actually led to the action.[5]

Permissibility: An explanation is permissible if and only if the action so explained violates no moral or practical requirement. Practical requirements are given by the purposes for which a CI system is designed.[6]

[3]An accurate explanation that reveals that the system's action is impermissible may also allow us to reduce its negative impact on us. Further, accurate explanations enable the system's engineers to improve it.

[4]Cf. (Armstrong et al., 2012) and (Weinberger, 2017).

[5]As this goes to show, rationalizing explanations are *a species* of causal explanation.

[6]We have to leave to one side difficulties arising from the fact that the same action can be described in different ways. See (Anscombe, 1962). Putting these in, we get: An explanation E is permissible iff the action explained by it *under a description*

Graspability: An explanation is graspable for some person P if and only if the explanation makes use only of concepts P can grasp.

To be ideally trustworthy, a CI system needs to provide us with a rationalizing explanation which is accurate, graspable, and permissible.

3 Two Challenges for CI Trustworthiness

But how do we connect this result to the actual workings of CI systems? We use an example of a simple mechanism that sorts integers to illustrate two challenges in designing trustworthy CI systems. Let $sort$ be an arbitrary but correct sorting mechanism for lists of integers. For instance, an invocation of $sort$ on input $[3, 5, 0]$ gives output $[0, 3, 5]$.

How can we explain this output? Rationalizing explanations appeal to the *goals* that the system pursues and the *information* that it used to determine how to achieve them. A goal can be understood in terms of a specification of desired outputs, given an input. Here is a specification for *sort* using the standard model of integers: The successor of each integer within the output list, if present, is greater-equal than its predecessor and the output list contains the same integers as the input list.

3.1 The Permissibility-Accuracy Challenge

The need for goals and information raises the *Permissibility-Accuracy Challenge for CI trustworthiness*. We can give a high-level description of the goal to be set for the system: 'Choose the best applicant!'. But—unlike in the case of the *sort*—we don't know what exactly our high-level description means in terms of an input/output specification. By training the system we hope that it develops its own conception of the characteristics of a good applicant. This is what makes CI systems so powerful, but also what makes them problematic. For we cannot be sure whether a system is trained with our intended goals. Nor can we know for certain what information guides its action, so we cannot be sure whether its *actual* goals and information are permissible. To achieve trustworthiness for CI systems, then, we need to gain access to the actual goals and the information, or at least to know whether they really are permissible. As argued in Sect. 2.2, for establishing trust, it is insufficient to have *some* permissible explanation of the decision in question that doesn't reflect the actual decision-making process.

3.2 The Graspability-Accuracy Challenge

Next, it should be possible to infer from a protocol of the internal processing of the system to the information used by it to achieve its goal. In case of a classical sorting algorithm, the protocol consists of the individual symbolic steps executed.

By contrast, subsymbolic protocols of the internal processing of CI systems are not protocols of symbolic steps executed within the system, corresponding to, for instance, concepts of integer comparison or arithmetic. Rather, they provide accurate merely causal explanations, but are useless for providing rationalizing explanations. For we cannot make much sense of information presented in such monolithic form. This constitutes the *second challenge for CI trustworthiness*: We need to be able to extract or infer the information which determined the result, but also the system's *actual* goals, in terms of concepts we can grasp. As before, trustworthiness requires more than just some graspable though made-up explanation.

4 How to Meet the Challenges

To achieve CI trustworthiness, we need to tackle the two challenges: acquire rationalizing explanations which are both accurate—particularly with respect to their permissibility status—and graspable. In the following we will sketch, in a 'black box' kind of way, a mechanism that could be used to generate such explanations for CI behavior.

Formally, an accurate rationalizing explanation E consists of a set of goals G and the information which is used to determine how to achieve these goals Λ, i.e., $E := \langle G, \Lambda \rangle$. Furthermore E appeals to a model M_E which provides the concepts used within the explanation.[7] Moreover, let C denote some CI system, trained with some data D, resulting in an internal inaccessible model M and goals G. Let O_I be the output generated by C on some

matching the explanation violates no moral or practical requirement.

[7]Think of the model as including the general information about the world the system possesses, which is coached in the concepts possessed by the system.

input I. E explains O_I with respect to I if and only if it makes the output rationally intelligible.

To obtain an accurate and graspable rationalizing explanation E (or something close enough) we propose the following mechanism:

First, we need to build a *Confabulator.* Given solely an input/output series, it constructs explanatory hypotheses, i.e., candidate goals G_C and corresponding candidate explanations $E_C := \langle G_C, \Lambda_C \rangle$ appealing to a candidate model M_C which is graspable, i.e., contains only concepts we can grasp, which makes E_C graspable as well.[8] The resulting candidate explanations ignore the inaccessible actual internal model M and the actual goals G. For instance, for *sort,* we can obtain candidate explanations E_1 and E_2 based on the standard model of integers $M_{\mathbb{N}}$ and a candidate goal, which is in this case the specification S, given above:

$$E_1 : \langle S, 0 < 3; 3 < 5 \rangle \qquad E_2 : \langle S, 0 < 3; 5 > 3 \rangle$$

The Confabulator's candidate explanations have a serious shortcoming: If they are accurate at all, this is pure luck. How do we know whether $M_{\mathbb{N}}$ and the relations of *greater-than* and *less-than* play any role in the actual decision making process? Say the candidate are constructed based on a series of input lists already sorted in reverse order—if so, the mechanism could equally well have the goal of reversing lists instead of sorting them. Typically, for actual CI systems, we don't even have any specification at hand and, thus, don't know the goals. The same goes for the automated hiring system. Here, the Confabulator need to guess—or learn—the goals.

Generally, there can be multiple, mutually exclusive candidate explanations which explain the same input/output series by appeal to different goals and models, where only some of these candidate explanations are *permissible.* We call this phenomenon *explanatory underdetermination.* This can be a severe problem, e.g., there may be multiple candidate explanations of the applicant ranking, of which only some are permissible, and at the same time we are unable to verify the system directly, for we lack a specification.

[8]The Confabulator may consist of human experts, of some additional system with or without access to the system under consideration, or be part of the CI system itself.

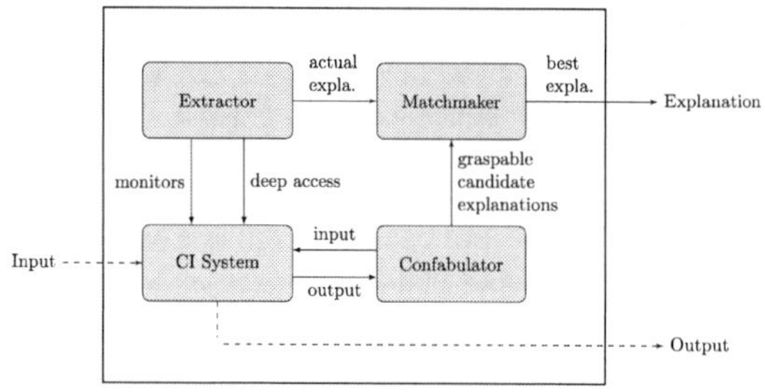

Figure 1: The configuration and interplay of a CI system with Extractor, Confabulator and Matchmaker.

This is where the second part of our proposed mechanism comes in: The *Extractor.* It extracts the Actual Explanation of the CI system's action which is probably not *graspable,* but can presumably be given, e.g., as a subsymbolic execution protocol preceding the action. The Actual Explanation may be of the wrong kind—merely causal instead of rationalizing—, but, from it, it should in principle be possible to extract or infer the reasons for which the system acted.

As a third part of the proposed mechanism, we then add a *Matchmaker,* a mechanism which matches the Extractor's ungraspable accurate explanation with the Confabulator's graspable, at best luckily accurate candidate explanations, and which then outputs a Best Explanation as *the* explanation of the CI system's decision. In so doing, the Matchmaker accords to the following principles:

(Im)permissibility Preservation: The Best Explanation is permissible if and only if the Actual Explanation is permissible.

Explanatory Equivalence: The Best Explanation is explanatory equivalent to the Actual Explanation: Any output that can be explained, on the basis of the Actual Explanation and in the light of a given input, is explainable by the Best Explanation in the light of the same input.

What allows for the possibility of the Matchmaker is that there is explanatory underdetermination. Seeing as there can be more than one explanation of the same action, we can try to move from an ungraspable actual and thus accurate explanation to a corresponding graspable explanation which preserves the permissibility status of the actual explanation. By additionally requiring Explanatory Equivalence, we get accuracy—or something close enough.[9]

5 Conclusion

We have argued that for trustworthiness, CI systems have to do more than 'just their job': they have to do what they are entrusted to do for permissible reasons and to give rationalizing explanations of their behavior which are accurate and graspable. We supported this claim by drawing parallels with trustworthy human persons, and by applying our claims to a hypothetical CI hiring system. We then presented two challenges for designing trustworthy CI systems. Finally, we sketched a mechanism consisting of three components—a Confabulator, an Extractor and a Matchmaker—which could be used to generate sufficiently accurate and graspable rationalizing Best Explanations for CI behavior.[10]

This may not be the only architecture to overcome the fundamental challenges of trustworthy CI design. Difficult obstacles along the way to building our proposed mechanism are to be expected.[11] However, we believe that trying out concrete and feasible proposals for building explainable CI systems is essential to making any progress in this area at all. So, designing the three components of our proposed mechanism should be high on the research agenda of those interested in explainable CI.

References

Elizabeth Anscombe. 1962. *Intention*. Harvard University Press, Cambridge, MA.

Stuart Armstrong, Anders Sandberg, and Nick Bostrom. 2012. Thinking inside the box: Controlling and using an oracle ai. *Minds and Machines*, 22(4):299–324.

Aylin Caliskan, Joanna J. Bryson, and Arvind Narayanan. 2017. Semantics derived automatically from language corpora contain human-like biases. *Science*, 356(6334):183–186.

Donald Davidson. 1963. Actions, reasons, and causes. *Journal of Philosophy*, 60:685–700.

Immanuel Kant. 1997. *Groundwork of the Metaphysics of Morals*. Cambridge University Press, Cambridge.

Carolyn McLeod. 2015. Trust. In Edward N. Zalta, editor, *The Stanford Encyclopedia of Philosophy (Fall 2015 Edition)*. Stanford University.

David Weinberger. 2017. Alien knowledge: When machines justify knowledge.

[9]We have to leave out our detailed, Anscombe-inspired account of what makes a Best Explanation sufficiently accurate.

[10]Most likely, one component will fulfill all three roles at once. Note that our proposed system can use explicit *requests* for explanations as constraints on the Confabulator's output. E.g., when we want to ensure that the applicant rating CI system isn't biased against black people, we can ask the Confabulator to confabulate explanations that involve that kind of bias and then try to match it using the Matchmaker with the actual explanation extracted by the Extractor.

[11]Here's one: How can we be certain that the components of our Best Explanation Generator are trustworthy?

A Simple Method for Clarifying Sentences with Coordination Ambiguities

Michael White and **Manjuan Duan** and **David L. King**
Department of Linguistics
The Ohio State University
Columbus, OH 43210 USA
mwhite@ling.osu.edu, {duan.59,king.2138}@osu.edu

Abstract

We present a simple, broad coverage method for clarifying the meaning of sentences with coordination ambiguities, a frequent cause of parse errors. For each of the two most likely parses involving a coordination ambiguity, we produce a disambiguating paraphrase that splits the sentence in two, with one conjunct appearing in each half, so that the span of each conjunct becomes clearer. In a validation study, we show that the method enables meaning judgments to be crowd-sourced with good reliability, achieving 83% accuracy at 80% coverage.

1 Introduction

In principle, intelligent systems should be capable of explaining how they have interpreted unrestricted natural language sentences. Although some early dialogue systems such as SHRDLU (Winograd, 1973) could ask questions to clarify the meaning of certain structurally ambiguous sentences, little work has been done to date on the task of generating questions to clarify structural ambiguities in a broad coverage setting. Recently, Duan et al. (2016) have shown that generating unambiguous paraphrases from competing parses of structurally ambiguous sentences can serve as a useful method for asking to clarify their intended meaning; in particular, they showed that their method enables crowd-sourced meaning judgments to be collected in order to improve parser accuracy in new domains. Duan et al.'s study covered most of the major sources of common parser errors identified by Kummerfeld et al. (2012), with the exception of ambiguities involving the correct spans of conjuncts in coordinated phrases (unless they involve modifier attachment ambiguities). Also closely related is He et al.'s (2016) work on generating questions to identify semantic roles, though their work does not address coordination span ambiguities either.

In this paper, we present a novel method for generating disambiguating paraphrases for sentences with ambiguities involving two coordinated elements where the sentence is split in two, with one conjunct appearing in each half, so that the span of each conjunct becomes clearer. In a validation study, we show that the method enables meaning judgments to be crowd-sourced with good reliability. Following an error analysis that highlights problematic cases, we conclude with a discussion of ways in which the method could be improved.

2 Disambiguation Method

At a high level, our method for generating disambiguating paraphrases for sentences with coordination ambiguities is as follows:

1. Parse the sentence and determine whether the most likely parse (henceforth the 'top' parse) has a coordinated phrase with two conjuncts/disjuncts, recording its span in words.

2. Examine the subsequent parses in the n-best list (in order) to determine whether the parse (henceforth the 'next' parse) has a coordinated phrase with a different span.

3. If such 'top' and 'next' parses are found, generate paraphrases by

Proceedings of the 1st Workshop on Explainable Computational Intelligence, pages 6–10, Santiago de Compostela, Spain, September 4 2017.

```
(w1 / do [mood=dcl tense=pres]
 :Arg0 (w0 / they)
 :Arg1 (w2 / have
        :Arg0 w0
        :Arg1 (w5 / selection [num=sg]
               :Det (w3 / a)
               :Mod (w4 / good)
               :Mod (w6 / of
                     :Arg1 (w8 / and
                            :First (w7 / fabric
                                     [det=nil num=sg])
                            :Next (w9 / notion
                                    [det=nil num=pl]))))))
```

(a) Semantic dependency graph of 'top' parse

```
(w1 / do [mood=dcl tense=pres]
 :Arg0 (w0 / they)
 :Arg1 (w2 / have
        :Arg0 w0
        :Arg1 (w8 / and
               :First (w5 / selection [num=sg]
                       :Det (w3 / a)
                       :Mod (w4 / good)
                       :Mod (w6 / of
                             :Arg1 (w7 / fabric
                                     [det=nil num=sg])))
               :Next (w9 / notion [det=nil num=pl]))))
```

(b) Semantic dependency graph of 'next' parse

Figure 1: Most likely parses for (1)

(a) copying the words up to and including the first conjunct, followed by the words following the coordinated phrase;

(b) copying any sentence-final punctuation, then starting a new sentence by copying the conjunction; and

(c) again copying the words up to the first conjunct, then copying the second conjunct, again followed by the words following the coordinated phrase.

To illustrate, consider (1) below, a sentence from the English Web Treebank,[1] a corpus which is primarily out-of-domain for parsers trained on the original Penn Treebank. This sentence has a coordination ambiguity between *a good selection of [[fabric] and [notions]]* and *[[a good selection of fabric] and [notions]]*, which is not (conventionally) analyzed as a modifier attachment ambiguity.[2]

(1) They do have a good selection of fabric and notions.

a. They do have a good selection of fabric. And they do have a good selection of notions.

b. They do have a good selection of fabric. And they do have notions.

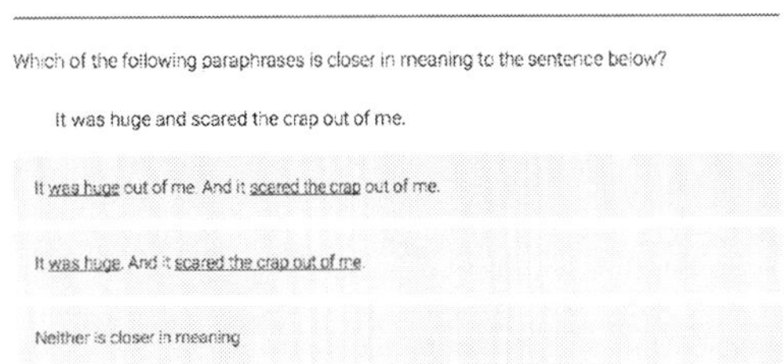

Figure 2: Sample survey question

The disambiguating paraphrase for the former, 'top' parse (correct according to the English Web Treebank) appears in (1-a), and the one for the latter, 'next' parse appears in (1-b), with underlining to highlight the differences between them.

To parse sentences, we use the Berkeley parser (Petrov et al., 2006) trained on OpenCCG[3] derivations (White, 2006; White et al., 2007; Boxwell and White, 2008) extracted from the CCGbank (Hockenmaier and Steedman, 2007). Derivations yield semantic dependency graphs represented using Hybrid Logic Dependency Semantics; the dependency graphs for (1) appear in Figure 1 using AMR-style notation (Banarescu et al., 2013). As shown in the figure, the `:First` and `:Next` relations can be used to identify coordinated phrases, and word identifiers allow spans to be extracted from subtrees.[4]

3 Crowd-Sourcing Judgments

We used Amazon Mechanical Turk (AMT) to crowd-source meaning judgments using our method of paraphrasing coordination ambiguities. Workers were given no training and very simple instructions, namely to select the paraphrase that is closer

[1]https://catalog.ldc.upenn.edu/ldc2012t13

[2]Note that sentences with ambiguities involving post-modifiers are dealt with symmetrically.

[3]http://openccg.sourceforge.net/

[4]Note that the conjunct spans can be accurately obtained even for shared argument coordination, e.g. VP-coordination or right node raising. Also note that as an alternative to the simple, surface-level algorithm employed here, we could have made changes to the dependency graphs and used OpenCCG to realize the modified graphs back as two sentences, which could avoid occasional errors with subject-verb agreement; the advantage of the present method is that it ensures that no undesired changes are made elsewhere in the sentence, as can happen with a broad coverage surface realizer.

Coverage	Accuracy			
	Majority		MACE	
	All	w/ Excl.	All	Filtered
25%	1.00	-	1.00	1.00
35%	-	0.98	0.97	1.00
50%	0.93	-	0.89	0.91
60%	-	0.88	0.87	0.90
80%	-	-	**0.83**	**0.84**
100%	0.75	0.75	0.74	-

Table 1: Coverage vs. accuracy highlights using majority vote (majority, strong majority, near unanimity) and MACE with all workers; majority vote with poorly performing workers excluded; and MACE with 'neither' responses filtered out

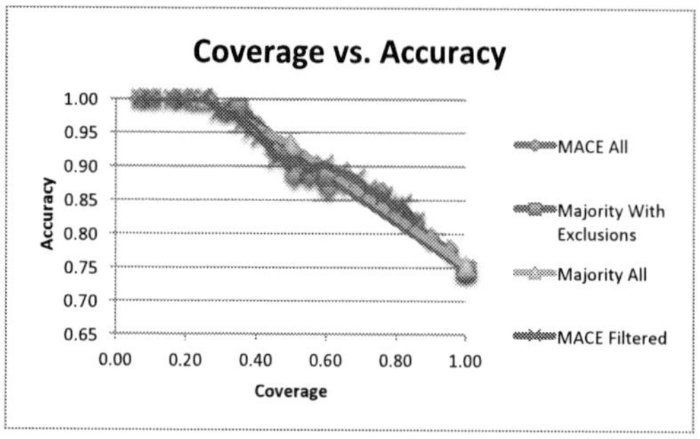

Figure 3: Coverage vs. accuracy using majority vote (majority, strong majority, near unanimity) and MACE across various confidence levels

in meaning to the original sentence, even it does not mean exactly the same thing, or 'neither' if neither sentence is closer in meaning. A screen shot showing a survey question appears in Figure 2.

For our validation experiment, we generated paraphrases for 172 items taken from the development section of the English Web Treebank. From these 172 items, twelve that were relatively short and clear were selected to be control items. The items were randomly distributed across eight surveys, with each survey containing 28 items, of which eight were control items, with four items per page.

We sought five workers to complete each survey. Workers were required to have a US IP address, be native speakers of English, and have achieved Masters status on AMT. Workers were told that they needed to get 75% of the control items correct. For five of the eight surveys, one worker failed to achieve 75% correct on the control items, so we sought an additional worker for each of these. All workers were paid $2 per survey, including the ones who failed to reach 75% on the control items, as they did not appear to be answering randomly. Each survey took 10-15 minutes to complete.

4 Results

4.1 Coverage vs. Accuracy

We measured the accuracy of the crowd-sourced judgments against our own expert judgments at various coverage levels. The results appear in Table 1 and Figure 3. Unlike the crowd-sourced judgments, our expert judgments were based on examining the 'top' and 'next' parses to see which one (if any) was more correct, consulting the structure annotated in the English Web Treebank in cases with any doubt.

One way to aggregate crowd-sourced judgments across multiple annotators is to simply take the majority judgment, breaking ties randomly. In this case, a consensus judgment is obtained for all items, so coverage is 100%. As shown in the table, accuracy at this coverage level is 75%, much higher than the chance level of 33.3%. A trade-off between coverage and accuracy can also be obtained by requiring a super-majority: for a strong majority, we required at least 75% agreement, and for (near) unanimity, we required at least 90% agreement. When all annotators are included—even those who performed poorly on the control items—requiring a strong majority reduces coverage to only 50%, but accuracy goes up to 93%; with the poorly performing annotators excluded, there are more strong majority cases, with 60% coverage, but accuracy is relatively lower, at 88%. Requiring (near) unanimity reduces coverage further, but raises accuracy to near 100%.

As an alternative to using majority judgments, MACE[5] (Hovy et al., 2013) can be used to make consensus predictions by weighting annotator judgments by their competence, where competence is estimated using expectation maximization. These consensus predictions can be assigned a confidence value according not only to agreement but also to estimated annotator competence. We ran MACE with thresholds to retain only the 5%, 10%, 15%,

[5]Multi-Annotator Competence Estimation

Error type	Count
preceding modifier scope ambiguity	14
following modifier scope ambiguity	4
apposition	4
miscellaneous	8
'neither' cases	14
total errors	44

Table 2: Distribution of errors

. . . 100% of the items with the highest model confidence, as shown in the figure; with MACE, it made little difference whether poorly performing annotators were excluded, so we only show the results with all annotators here. The accuracy of the MACE-derived consensus judgments was no better than with the majority judgments, but MACE did make it possible to identify a sweet spot where coverage is still high at 80% while accuracy is substantially higher at 83% than in the full-coverage case. Finally, the table and figure also show the coverage and accuracy when items where 'neither' was the consensus judgment are excluded, as these would be unhelpful for parser adaptation: here, a slightly higher accuracy of 84% is attained at the 80% coverage level.

4.2 Error Analysis

The distribution of errors using MACE at the 100% coverage level appears in Table 2. Out of 172 items, the annotator consensus differed from our judgment in 44 cases. Most of the errors were related to either modification or apposition. The miscellaneous errors were ones that only occurred once. There were also 7 items where neither parse was more correct, and 7 where the annotator consensus was erroneously 'neither', typically because parse errors led to hard-to-understand paraphrases.

Of the 30 remaining (non-'neither') errors, roughly half involved preceding modifiers with ambiguous scope. Although our paraphrasing method handles preceding modifiers within noun phrases reasonably well, adverbial scope proved more difficult to disambiguate. For example, consider (2):

(2) So go and get dancing!!!!!!!!!!!!!!!!!!!!!!!!.

a. So go![...]. And so get dancing![...].

b. So go![...]. And get dancing![...].

Although without context, it is somewhat difficult to tell whether the scope of the discourse connective *so* applies to both imperative clauses or only the first, our crowd sourced annotators overwhelmingly preferred the paraphrase (3-b) of the 'next' parse, contrary to the English Web Treebank. One possible reason is that here, repeating *so* in (3-a) is quite awkward. Additionally, although *so* is only in the first sentence of paraphrase (3-b), it is easy to interpret it as also modifying the second clause.

Of the remaining errors, paraphrases from appositive constructions such as (3) stood out, as these do not have a straightforwardly distributive interpretation. Likewise, there were a couple errors involving collective readings for conjoined noun phrases.

(3) Shuttle veteran and longtime NASA executive Fred Gregory is temporarily at the helm of the 18,000-person agency.

a. Shuttle veteran is temporarily at the helm of the 18,000-person agency. And long time NASA executive Fred Gregory is temporarily at the helm of the 18,000-person agency.

b. Shuttle veteran is temporarily at the helm of the 18,000-person agency. And shuttle long time NASA executive Fred Gregory is temporarily at he helm of the 18,000-person agency.

5 Discussion

Our validation study has shown that our simple, broad coverage method for clarifying the meaning of sentences with coordination ambiguities enables meaning judgments to be crowd-sourced with good reliability, far above chance and at a level that can be expected to pay off for parser domain adaptation. Since the method is so simple, it should be possible to adapt to a variety of parsing frameworks.

Not surprisingly, an error analysis revealed that sentences whose interpretations are not straightforwardly distributive are problematic for our method, indicating that a more sophisticated way to handle such sentences is required. Less obviously, adverbial pre-modifiers turned out to work relatively poorly, suggesting that Duan et al.'s (2016) method for disambiguating these represents a better option.

Acknowledgments

We thank the OSU Clippers Group and the anonymous reviewers for helpful comments and discussion. This work was supported in part by NSF grant IIS-1319318.

References

Laura Banarescu, Claire Bonial, Shu Cai, Madalina Georgescu, Kira Griffitt, Ulf Hermjakob, Kevin Knight, Philipp Koehn, Martha Palmer, and Nathan Schneider. 2013. Abstract Meaning Representation for Sembanking. In *Proceedings of the 7th Linguistic Annotation Workshop and Interoperability with Discourse*, pages 178–186. Association for Computational Linguistics.

Stephen Boxwell and Michael White. 2008. Projecting Propbank roles onto the CCGbank. In *Proc. LREC-08*.

Manjuan Duan, Ethan Hill, and Michael White. 2016. Generating disambiguating paraphrases for structurally ambiguous sentences. In *Proceedings of the 10th Linguistic Annotation Workshop held in conjunction with ACL 2016 (LAW-X 2016)*, pages 160–170. Association for Computational Linguistics.

Luheng He, Julian Michael, Mike Lewis, and Luke Zettlemoyer. 2016. Human-in-the-loop parsing. In *Proceedings of the 2016 Conference on Empirical Methods in Natural Language Processing*, pages 2337–2342. Association for Computational Linguistics.

Julia Hockenmaier and Mark Steedman. 2007. CCGbank: A Corpus of CCG Derivations and Dependency Structures Extracted from the Penn Treebank. *Computational Linguistics*, 33(3):355–396.

Dirk Hovy, Taylor Berg-Kirkpatrick, Ashish Vaswani, and Eduard Hovy. 2013. Learning whom to trust with MACE. In *Proceedings of the 2013 Conference of the North American Chapter of the Association for Computational Linguistics: Human Language Technologies*, pages 1120–1130. Association for Computational Linguistics.

Jonathan K. Kummerfeld, David Hall, James R. Curran, and Dan Klein. 2012. Parser showdown at the wall street corral: An empirical investigation of error types in parser output. In *Proceedings of the 2012 Joint Conference on Empirical Methods in Natural Language Processing and Computational Natural Language Learning*, pages 1048–1059, Jeju Island, South Korea, July. Association for Computational Linguistics.

Slav Petrov, Leon Barrett, Romain Thibaux, and Dan Klein. 2006. Learning accurate, compact, and interpretable tree annotation. In *Proceedings of COLING-ACL*.

Michael White, Rajakrishnan Rajkumar, and Scott Martin. 2007. Towards broad coverage surface realization with CCG. In *Proc. of the Workshop on Using Corpora for NLG: Language Generation and Machine Translation (UCNLG+MT)*.

Michael White. 2006. Efficient Realization of Coordinate Structures in Combinatory Categorial Grammar. *Research on Language & Computation*, 4(1):39–75.

Terry Winograd. 1973. A procedural model of language understanding. In Roger Schank and Ken Colby, editors, *Computer Models of Thought and Language*, pages 152–186. W.H. Freeman. Reprinted in Grosz et al. (eds), Readings in Natural Language Processing. Los Altos CA: Morgan Kaufmann Publishers, 1986, pp.249-266.

Requirements for Conceptual Representations of Explanations and How Reasoning Systems Can Serve Them

Helmut Horacek
helmut.horacek@dfki.de

Abstract

Explanations of solutions produced by reasoning systems in ever growing complexity become increasingly interesting, which is particularly challenging in view of fundamental differences between human and machine representation and problem-solving methods. In this paper, we formulate requirements for conceptual representations that are adequate for producing human-oriented explanations, and we discuss how some reasoning mechanisms can serve them or can possibly be adapted to do so. This examination is intended to state in what ways reasoning systems can potentially support explanation generation, and where technology-justified limitations have to be accepted.

1 Introduction

Explanations justifying or questioning results produced by intelligent systems were always of interest, but this issue was rarely addressed in depth. Simple attempts with expert systems, although being one of the most explanation-friendly reasoning techniques, produced unexpectedly poor results, mainly because of insufficient understanding of impacts of human expectations and inference capabilities in discourse. This situation motivated the ambitious approach to *Explainable Expert Systems* (EES) (Swartout, Smoliar, 1997). The idea is to treat explanation not as an „afterthought" but to foresee possible extra demands of explanations by incorporating suitable „built-ins" within the reasoning process. While this strategy turned out to be successful for expert systems, it hardly looks promising for many other categories of reasoning systems where the discrepancy to human-like reasoning is considerably more pronounced.

An intellectual challenge has been mastered recently by a system that has beaten the human champion of Go in a match (Silver et al. 2016). The system applied deep neural network learning and searching on the basis of enormously large amount of data, that is, millions of games. While this is sufficient to outperform top level players in the purely performance-oriented task of a match, the system, similar to chess programs, cannot document its behavior in human-relevant terms, because it does not have an explicit representation of most domain-relevant concepts, which form the basis for human-adequate explanations.

Motivated by this gap between machine and human representation concepts, we formulate requirements for conceptual representations that are adequate for producing human-oriented explanations, and we discuss how some prominent reasoning mechanisms can serve them or can possibly be adapted to do so. Reasoning techniques referred to include rule-based representations, constraint-systems, decision trees, Bayesian networks and neural networks.

This paper is organized as follows. We first investigate what is required for producing explanations that are likely to be meaningful and useful to humans, and we formulate a set of complementary requirements. Then we examine some major reasoning techniques from the perspective of how they can serve explanation-motivated requirements, and if there is a gap, how it can possibly be narrowed. We also briefly address issues of natural-language presentation. Finally, we discuss the state-of affairs and expected future developments.

2 Requirements for Explanations

In this section, we discuss what is needed to provide representations from which human-adequate explanations can reasonably be generated with linguistic techniques. We focus on representations here because most linguistic presentation techniques needed to map these representations onto text are suitable for several genres of text. In addition, we devote a short section to specificities of explanations, such as the role of implicit conveyance of information, towards the end of the paper.

Proceedings of the 1st Workshop on Explainable Computational Intelligence, pages 11–15, Santiago de Compostela, Spain, September 4 2017.

2.1 Categories for Explanations

Explanations may come in a variety of forms serving in part quite complementary purposes, mostly depending on the task at hand: this may be some proof of evidence for a solution, investigating constellations that may qualify for a solution, inquiring rationals for classification or decision preferences. We distinguish five categories of explanations:

1. *Exposition of the lines of reasoning*
This kind of explanations addresses the adequate presentation of an inference chain, more general a tree or graph of inferences, be it in the context of a theorem prover, an expert system, or an argumentation framework. The purpose is to increase confidence in results obtained by a system, which may be by verifying the overall course of solution, or by referring to essential ingredients.
2. *Hypothetical inquiries*
This kind of explanation is typically revelant for situations in which expectations or user beliefs are not met by solutions proposed by a system. Users may have interest in some specific constellation which turned out to be inferior or unacceptable, may be due to some small detail, or it may simply be unexplored. It is desirable for this kind of explanation to focus on essential reasons.
3. *Justification for categorization*
This kind of explanation refers to the ingredients that have contributed to a taxonomic decision. As with the previous category, focusing on essential factors rather than on completeness is of importance here; thereby, possible reasons for misconceptons may be met, which may have motivated the explanatory request.
4. *Decision preferences*
This kind of explanation refers to a comparison between properties of an entity in question and its closest competitors in the decision, or some explicitly mentioned candidates. In terms of what is to be compared, a combination of the previous and the following category may apply.
5. *Issues of calculation*
This component of explanation focuses on impacts of quantitative properties and their dependencies on the issue to be explained. A detailed exposition of all calculations is of minor importance – simple ranges of numbers are preferable, including justification where they come from.

There are larger and richer catalogs of categories, but we think that we have captured the most principled ones. One important category missing are meta-explanations, about problem-solving strategies and their application, but this is a weakness of virtually all systems, since they do not have explicit representations of how they are working.

2.2 Properties of Human-Adequate Explanations

In order for representations to be suitable for explanations we think some criteria are indispensible:

1 *Focused content*
For an explanation to be useful, its content must be to the point of the purpose of the explanatory request. It is of little help if the content is somehow related to what is expected as an explanation. If the reasoning mechanism does not enable building an adequate response specification, we feel it is better to provide partial or incomplete information or evidence that may be not optimal.
2 *Vocabulary used*
The content provided should be expressed in terms the audience is familiar with. By this requirement, we do not mean a difference between expert and novice terminology, which can be bridged by natural language generation techniques, at least to some degree. The requirement addresses those cases where the problem-solving technique used by machines is fundamentally different from human approaches – human domain concepts are not used and may not easily be identifiable if at all within the machines' approach.
3 *Granularity*
The content of an explanation should be expressed in an adequate level of detail. If it is too detailed, an overall explanation may be longish and perceived as boring, and may even get incomprehensible. If it does not contain enough details, it may not be of use due to limited information.

3 Examining Explanation Potentials for Problem-Solving Techniques

In this section, we discuss to what extent the criteria elaborated in the previous subsection can be met by some major reasoning techniques, and we discuss measures to increase coverage and quality.

3.1 Systems with Rule-like Representations

This category comprises expert systems, automated theorem provers, and argumentation frameworks. These systems can serve the content of explanations for exposition of the lines of reasoning rather well. Similarly, the vocabulary and level of granularity is widely in accordance with human reasoning, except to automated theorem provers. They almost exclusively operate on the detailed resolution calculus, where the connection to the originally specified mathematical axioms, which constitute the basic vocabulary in this domain, gets widely lost. Fortunately, there are automated transformation procedures which can lift the proof representation to the more abstract *assertion level* (Huang, 1994).

An exception are cognitively involved inference patterns, such as modus tollens and disjunction elimination – several of these are composed into an assertion level step – a decomposition into natural deduction level steps is advisable (Horacek 1998, 1999, 2007). Some domain rules in expert systems may be associated with annotations that express their justification, much in the style of EES. Explanations on a higher level of granularity, such as as proof sketches and proof ideas are essentially unexplored. Skeletons of proofs plans may be adapted for this purpose, but such approaches are rare.

3.2 Constraint Systems

For this category of systems, the suitability for explanations appears to be rather good, at first sight. For typical applications, constraints themselves are expressed on a level corresponding to human views, so that vocabulary and granularity can be expected to be on a suitable level. May be, there are higher-level conceptions which correspond to a set or some composition of several constraints, so that addressing the more abstract view requires some transformation process to take place, possibly on demand by a specific explanatory request. Potential problems with explanations become only clearer when explanatory requests and information produced by the problem-solving techniques are put in relation to one another. Requests for justifying a solution are not of major interest for constraint systems; the simple explanation is just a message indicating that all constraints are fulfilled for the solution proposed. More informative messages would selectively list those constraints which are barely fulfilled, for constraints which involve a numerical comparison. In addition, a meta-explanation about the portion of the search space explored and the degree to which optimality is approached may be suitable, in case the system is set up in a way so that search is stopped when a solution with satisfactory quality is foumd. However, describing the search space in terms of which portions are still unexplored may be quite demanding.

Another category of explanations suitable for problems addressed by constraints systems are hypothetical inquiries. In a design problem, several inquiries may refer to partial constellations which the designer might expect or prefer to be part of a solution, but the system results show different combinations. In an explanation the reasons might be some violated set of constraints, but this information might not necessarily be complete or best. For excluding some combination of values from being a solution, a single constraint responsible for that is sufficient – in the search, every effort is made to exclude as much as possible on as little information as available. Hence, in order to obtain a more complete and focused view, checking and evaluating additional constraints for explanatory purposes only might prove suitable. An extreme approach for this purpose is described in (Horacek, 1992), which attempts to establishes dominances among sets of constraints, much in the style of Berliner (1979, 1982), but it requires full exploration of the search space. Altogether, explanations for constraint systems appear reasonably doable, but the content quality may not always be as desirable, and additional computation effort is required to address this issue.

3.3 Decision Trees

This problem-solving method is mostly suitable for obtaining categorizations or preferences between choices of some sort. Similar to constraint systems, (good) reasons for a possibly unexpected categorization, thus, a hypothetical solution are typical of interest. Conversely, major reasons for the categorization obtained are much more sensible here than a similar explanatory request in the conext of constraint systems. Structurally, the content of an explanation for a hypothetical solution is a description of the expressions of one of the choice points where the path to the category inquired is missed. Conversely, a complete description addressing a request for the categorization obtained comprises the expressions associated with all choice points on the path to that categorization. More focused explanations may choose a suitable one among the choice points in the first case and they may be selective in concentrating on conceptually more important ones in the second case.

In contrast to the previous two system categories, presenting the content of explanations may prove to be problematic here, since the expressions associated with the choice points may be quite complex, typically not corresponding to domain concepts meaningful to humans, since the overall tree structure is motivated by the goal of obtained a mostly balanced tree. Consequently, there is a serious problem in the vocabulary discrepancy between the components of decision trees and human domain conceptions. We are aware of only a single attempt to bridge this gap: in the domain of elementary chess pawn endings (king plus pawn versus king), decision trees were built to discriminate won from drawn positions (Michalski, Negri 1977). The tree learned on the basis of the board data only was compact, but its form was felt obscure by human players. When the building of choice point was biased by some force to use domain concepts, such as pawn square, king opposition, etc., the tree learned was structurally less optimal, but much better understandable to humans in terms of the discriminations made. This is a good example for explanations being a built-in, though in a different way as in EES.

Reasoning method	*Weakness*	*Measures*
Rules	Granularity	Transformations
Constraints	Content, in part	Extra searching
Decision trees	Vocabulary	Biasing vocabulary
Bayesian networks	Role of numbers	Quantitative versions
Neural networks.	Content (+others)	Sensitivity analysis

Table 1. Reasoning methods, their weak points in explanation, some measures against.

3.4 Bayesian Networks

In this category of systems, explanations may address generic or individual requests to the network. Generic requests concern the topology of the network, which comprises dependencies, justifications, and probabilities, possibly extended by annotations in the style of EES (e.g., giving sources or other details about the probabilities). Altogether, this is a presentation task pretty much on the lines of documenting rules, augmented by references to and descriptions of probabilities. Individual requests can be dealt with in more details. As far as the dependency of events is concerned, this amounts to a composition of rules, possibly in a tree. The extra component is the reference to and documentation of the probabilities associated with events and coocurrences of events. Merely listing the numerical data and the results of calculations is not difficult, but in some cases at least, there may be a better vocabulary in terms of qualitative assessments, as approximations. Such an approach has been undertaken in the context of argumentative presentations in natural language (Carenini, Moore, 2006), where the natural language descriptions were preferred by users to the precise graphical displays.

3.5 Neural Networks

This is clearly the most explanation-resistant technique described in this section. Its performance-oriented strength loses in explanation-related terms, since the important intermediate levels are not anywhere near a conceptual interpretation. Thus, the mathematical aspect is dominating, so that the architectural inspiration by the human brain somehow stops half way - the network learns how to perform, but does not produce explicit conceptions in the resulting representation. Consequently, there is virtually nothing that provides a basis for an explanation, only input and output data being on a level accessible to humans. Some more options are available for networks with a specific topology, such as gated networks (Zhao et al. 2017), where activations at intermediate levels can be visualized; but this techniques is probably suitable for a specific set of tasks only. What is remaining would be reruns with similar related data, to find out essential differences on some experimental basis. In addition, value differences between alternative output items could be used to refer to close competitors, e.g., near misses. However, how to orchestrate a reasonable set of recomputations effectively is ambitious.

A summmary of the reasoning techniques discussed, in terms of major weaknesses and meaures to potentially overcome them is given in Table 1_

4 Presentation Methods

Explanation presentation needs good sentence planning, including aggregation (Di Eugenio et al. 2005), and argumentation organization (Carenini, Moore, 2006). In addition, having a good command of explicitness and implicitness in presentation is of great importance in this genre (Horacek 1998, 2007), even more prominently in varions versions of the Digital Aristotle (Porter, 2007). Note that deliberately leaving portions of the content specification implicit is fundamentally different from selectivity in building content specifications: the latter means that they are not to be conveyed to the user, whereas the former is justified by the expectation that the audience is able to infer the content left implicit.

By and large, constellatons for leaving parts of content specification implicit are fairly well understood at a local level, such as the preference of modus brevis to fully exposed modus ponens presentations, straightforward taxonomic and action inferences, and expansion of known and mastered definitions. However, orchestrating the combination of several such constellations in a contextually adequate manner is still a widely unanswered question.

5 Conclusion and Discussion

In this paper, we have advocated in favor of necessary properties of representations that are suitable for specifics of explanations: the content, the vocabulary, and the level of granularity. We have discussed how these requirements are met or not met by some prominent reasoning mechanisms, We also have referred to measures already addressed and we have sketched some more ways to overcome existing discrepancies. Measures range from built-in methods to extra computations invoked by explanatory requests; they include transformation and enhancement of representations, and extra computations for parts not contributing to a solution.

Approaches to explanation require capabilities in several fields, such as automated theorem proving and NLP, which few researchers can cover. Nevertheless, increasing success and use of reasoning facilities will require a better documentation of their capabilities, especially for users who are sceptical towards machine-generated problem solutions.

References

(Berliner 1979)

H. Berliner, On the Construction of Evaluation Functions for Large Domains. In Proceedings of the *6th International Joint Conference on Artificial Intelligence*, 53-55, Tokyo, Japan, 1979.

(Berliner, Ackley 1982)

H. Berliner, and D. Ackley. The QBKG System: Generating Explanations from a Non-Discrete Knowledge Representation. In Proceedings of the *Second National Conference on Artificial Intel- ligence (AAAI-82)*, 213-216, Pittsburgh, Pennsylvania, 1982.

(Silver et al. 2016)

D. Silver, A. Huang, C. J. Maddison, A. Guez, L. Sifre, G. van den Driessche, J. Schrittwieser, I. Antonoglou, V. Panneershelvam, M. Lanctot, S. Dieleman, D. Grewe, J. Nham, N. Kalchbrenner, I. Sutskever, T. Lillicrap, M. Leach, K. Kavukcuoglu, T. Graepel and D. Hassabis. Mastering the Game of Go with Deep Neural Networks and Tree Search. *NATURE*, Vol. 529, 2016.

(Carenini, Moore 2006)

G. Carenini and J. D. Moore, Generating and evaluating evaluative arguments. *Artificial Intelligence* Vol. 170, 925-952, 2006.

(Di Eugenio et al. 2005)

B. Di Eugenio, D. Fossati, D. Yu, S. Haller, and M. Glass, Natural Language Generation for Intelligent Tutoring Systems: a case study, *12th International Conference on Artificial Intelligence in Education*, Amsterdam, The Netherlands, 2005.

(Horacek 1992)

H. Horacek, Explanations for Constraint Systems. In B. Neumann (ed.), Proceedings of the *10th European Conference of Artificial Intelligence (ECAI-92)*, 500-504, Vienna, Austria, 1992.

(Horacek 1998)

H. Horacek. Generating Inference-Rich Discourse Through Revisions of RST Trees. In Proceedings of the *Fifteenth National Conference on Artificial Intelligence* (*AAAI-98)*, 814-820, 1998.

(Horacek 1999)

H. Horacek. Presenting Proofs in a Human-Oriented Way. In H. Ganzinger (ed.), Proceedings of the *16th International Conference on Automated Deduction* (*CADE-16)*, LNAI 1632, Springer, 142-156, 1999.

(Horacek 2007)

H. Horacek How to Build Explanations of Automated Proofs: A Methodology and Requirements on Domain Representations. *ExaCt 2007*: 34-41 Explanation-Aware Computing, Papers from the 2007 AAAI Workshop, Vancouver, British Columbia, Canada, July 22-23, 2007. AAAI Technical Report WS-07-06, AAAI Press 2007,

(Huang 1994)

X, Huang. Reconstructing Proofs at the Assertional Level. In Proceedings of the *12th International Conference on Automated Deduction (CADE-94)*, 738-752, Nancy, France, 1994.

(Michalski, Negri 1977)

R. S. Michalski and P. Negri An experiment on inductive learning in chess endgames.. In E. W. Elcock. D. Michie (eds.), Machine Intelligence 8, 175-192, Ellis Horwood, 1977.

(Porter 2007)

B. Porter. A New Class of Knowledge Systems and their Explanation Requirements. Invited talk at the *ExaCt 2007 Workshop on Explanation-aware Computing at AAAI 2007*, Vancouver, Canada, 2007.

(Swartout , Smoliar 1997)

B. Swartout and S. Smoliar. On Making Expert Systems more like Experts, Experts Sytsms, Vol 4(3), 196-208, 1997.

(Zhao et al.)

Y. Zhao, N. Semuma, X, Shen, and A.Aizawa. A Gated Neural Network for Sentence Compression Using Linguistic Knowledge, In Proceedings of 22nd *NLDB* conference, 2017.

An Essay on Self-explanatory Computational Intelligence: A Linguistic Model of Data Processing Systems

Jose M. Alonso
Centro de Investigación en Tecnoloxías da Información (CiTIUS)
University of Santiago de Compostela,
Santiago de Compostela, Spain
josemaria.alonso.moral@usc.es

Gracian Trivino
Phedes Lab,
Asturias, Spain
gracian.trivino@phedes.com

Abstract

Computational processes are increasingly more powerful and complex but also more difficult to understand by humans. Considering that Natural Language is a suitable tool for describing human perceptions, building self-explanatory computational systems ready to communicate with humans in Natural Language becomes a hot challenge. Based on ideas taken from Cognitive Science, we propose a novel model to facilitate achieving this goal. We consider the computer as a metaphor of the mind and we use references from Philosophy, Neurology, Linguistics, Anthropology and Sociology to provide a structure of different components that allow coping with the complexity of generating linguistic descriptions about computational processes. We illustrate the use of this model with several examples.

1 Introduction

Currently, computational systems allow accessing huge amounts of data about the phenomena in their environment. Nevertheless, users and engineers demand tools to reduce the size and complexity of these data into more friendly tractable dimensions. We, human beings, use Natural Language for describing our perceptions and also for construing our experience (Halliday and Matthiessen, 1999).

Indeed, nowadays, computers can use Natural Language to generate linguistic descriptions of the complex phenomena in their environment. The new challenge (Gunning, 2016) is to build self-explanatory computational systems, i.e., computational systems able to describe linguistically their own functioning.

There are several related research lines dealing with Argument Technology (Walton et al., 2008), Natural Language Generation (Reiter and Dale, 2000) and more specifically with Linguistic Description of Data (Ramos-Soto et al., 2016). Moreover, we have already proved the benefits of using Natural Language for building explainable fuzzy systems (Alonso et al., 2017).

When we deal with describing computational processes, we need a way of representing the meaning of the related linguistic descriptions, i.e., a way of organizing and coping with their complexity that would make them easier to understand.

The work presented in this paper contributes to a long term research project, the so-called Linguistic Description of Complex Phenomena (Trivino and Sugeno, 2013). The main contribution of this paper is a systemic model of the process performed by human beings and computers as Data Processing Systems (DPS) for producing new information from input data. We propose to use this model to organize the meaning of linguistic descriptions about the different components of computational processes.

This is a general model including few processes associated with specific families of linguistic expressions. The model deals with a classification of the main DPS activities and the more adequate linguistic expressions to describe them. Here, we present only a brief description of the model components but hopefully enough to provide the reader with an insight about the possibilities of the idea.

In Section 2 we present some preliminary con-

Proceedings of the 1st Workshop on Explainable Computational Intelligence, pages 16–20, Santiago de Compostela, Spain, September 4 2017.

cepts which are required to understand the proposal drawn in Section 3. Section 4 provides some illustrative examples. Finally, conclusions and future work are sketched in Section 5.

2 Several Concepts from Cognitive Science

One of the main premises of Cognitive Science asserts that the computer can be considered a metaphor of the mind (Gardner, 1987). This metaphor can be used in both directions, the computer to create an idea of how the mind works but also we can use our knowledge about the mind to organize linguistic descriptions about how computers work. With this last regard we recall several ideas from disciplines belonging to Cognitive Science.

From Philosophy, according with Popper, the universe where humans beings live can be divided into three worlds (Popper and Eccles, 1977):

- The world of the physical objects (W1).
- The world of the perceived objects (W2).
- The world of the mental objects (W3).

From Neurology, according with (Damasio, 2003), Natural Evolution has built the hierarchical control system of the human behavior by aggregating step by step a series of successive layers:

- The primitive layer, located in the inner part of the brain, is dedicated to immune responses, basic reflexes and metabolic regulation.
- Control related with pain and pleasure.
- Control based on drives and motivations.
- Control based on emotions and feelings.
- On the top of this hierarchy of control mechanisms we have the rationality. This is part of the most evolved behavior control mechanism that is based on using Natural Language.

From Linguistics, Systemic Functional Linguistics (Halliday and Matthiessen, 1999) provides a classification of the human activities into four main types and subtypes:

- **Being**: (1) Identifying, (2) Ascribing, and (3) Existing.
- **Sensing**: (1) Seeing, (2) Feeling, (3) Thinking, and (4) Wanting.
- **Doing**: (1) Doing to/with, (2) Happening, and (3) Behaving.
- **Saying**: there are no subtypes here.

3 A Linguistic Model of Data Processing Systems

This section presents the main contribution in this paper. We apply a systemic approach inspired by the ideas introduced in Section 2. We have defined a model which describes the basic components that both humans and computers see as Data Processing Systems (DPS). Fig. 1 shows a data flow diagram of the model. Rectangles correspond to data structures and ovals represent processes. In the rest of the section we describe the main components in the model. First, Section 3.1 describes the data structures. Second, Section 3.2 introduces the processes.

3.1 Data Structures

3.1.1 External Phenomena (W1)

This is the external world that forms the system environment. Using their sensors, DPS try to obtain useful data that are needed to perform their goals. Notice that most of the phenomena in W1 are beyond the limits of human/computers perception and understanding capacities.

We identify two main components in this world: (1) *World of physical objects*, and (2) *World of cultural objects*.

The *World of physical objects* corresponds with the first world described by (Popper and Eccles, 1977). Both human body and robot hardware are part of this world which is only accessed through physical introspection (proprioceptive sense).

Currently, as a result of the civilization process, the environment from which DPS perceive relevant phenomena and they must make their decisions is not only physical but also cultural. We call this *World of cultural objects*. According with Anthropology (Tomasello, 1999) and Sociology (Berger and Luckmann, 2011) this world is built by humankind following the Natural Evolution and using Natural Language.

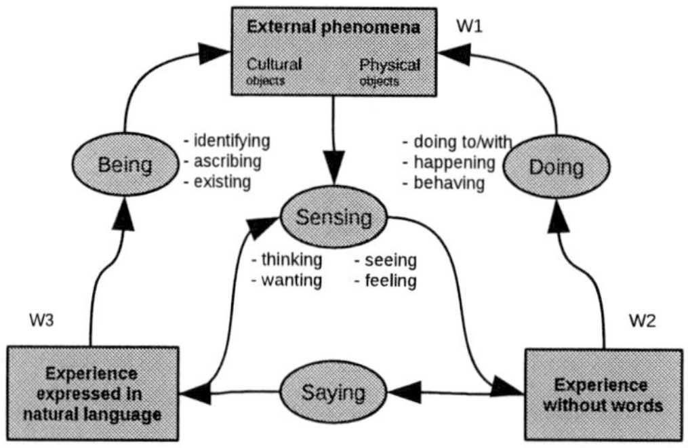

Figure 1: Data flow diagram of a linguistic model for Data Processing Systems (DPS).

3.1.2 Experience Without Words (W2)

It takes place in the internal world that is the domain of drives, emotions and feelings for humans. It is made up of internal images without words and corresponds with the Popper's second world, i.e., the world of the perceived objects. In computational systems, these objects are related to raw data, i.e., data that computers capture for driving reactive behaviors but that still need to be processed before becoming useful information. For example a video stream or a temporal series of temperatures coming out from a chemical process.

3.1.3 Experience Expressed in Natural Language (W3)

This data structure corresponds with the Popper's third world. In accordance with Neurology, it is part of the human consciousness (Damasio, 2010). The related information is produced in humans by using the rationality that is supported by the newest part of the human brain, the neocortex. This is part of the most evolved behavior control mechanism that is based on using the Natural Language. On the other hand, in computers, it is produced by using the highest levels of their computational architecture (Trivino et al., 2009).

3.2 Processes

It is noteworthy that the names of these processes are labels representing a classification (hierarchical structure) of possible linguistic expressions. During their application in the model, each specific situation will be described by using specific linguistic expressions belonging to these categories.

3.2.1 Sensing

This process allows DPS to obtain data about the *External phenomena*. *Seeing* is a specialized function or sensor (as sight, hearing, smell, taste, or touch in humans) by which DPS sense (obtain or receive) external or internal stimuli. It allows creating images of objects in the surrounding environment. With *Feeling* the system translates the information coming from external phenomena into emotions and feelings that will influence/condition the related behavior. In computers, it is used for reactive control. In Fig. 1 they correspond with the process *W1* $\rightarrow$ *W2*. *Thinking* and *Wanting* corresponds with the feedback *W3* $\rightarrow$ *W2*. DPS can distinguish between positively and negatively evaluated information and modify accordingly the related behavior. With *Saying* they close an internal control loop.

3.2.2 Doing

In Fig. 1, it corresponds with the process *W2* $\rightarrow$ *W1*. It includes the processes of physical acting and can be described by linguistic expressions like *Doing to/with*, *Happening*, and *Behaving*.

3.2.3 Saying

It is the process of generating linguistic descriptions of images or raw data. In Fig. 1, it corresponds with the process *W2* $\rightarrow$ *W3*. This is related to the research on Linguistic Descriptions of Complex Phenomena, e.g., (Conde-Clemente et al., 2017).

3.2.4 Being

In Fig. 1, it corresponds with the process *W3* $\rightarrow$ *W1*. It can be described by linguistic expressions like *Identifying*, *Ascribing*, and *Existing*. Using this process DPS create new objects and modify the objects in W1. Note that this is the mechanism used by DPS to send messages to other DPS.

4 Examples

In this section, with the aim of illustrating how to apply the model presented in Section 3, we describe briefly the sequences of processes followed in two examples of human behavior and in one example of computational processing.

4.1 Reactive Behavior

Let's suppose we observe a reactive behavior in a woman. She shows a typical reactive activity when the light of the sun is disturbing her to see something:

- She feels the sun on her eyes (sensing-seeing-feeling).
- She moves her head looking for the sun position (doing-behaving).
- She uses her hand to shadow her eyes (doing-doing with).

4.2 Deliberative Behavior

Here, the observed subject (a musician) shows a more sophisticated set of activities that consists of composing music:

- He listens to a bird through the window (sensing-seeing).
- He feels certain emotion (sensing-feeling).
- He plays the piano (doing-doing with).
- He expresses this music using the musical notation (saying).
- He publishes a piano score and makes the music available to others by creating a new object in their external world (being-existing).

4.3 Computational System Behavior

A computational system (DPS) monitors the movements of clients into a supermarket:

- It detects a change in the shopping entrance (Sensing).
- It changes the internal state to "detected new client" and stores the related image [experience without words].
- It moves the camera to follow the client (doing).
- It builds a map with different positions and timestamps (Saying).
- It detects the client is going out (Sensing).
- It sends a linguistic report to the store manager informing about business details (Being).

5 Conclusions

The presented model is the result of a multidisciplinary research and it is part of a long term project in the research line of Linguistic Descriptions of Complex Phenomena.

In general, computational processing of data are complex phenomena. The idea is that computers use a metaphor to describe their internal processes. The human user is helped to understand the computer processes by using the same terminology that the user uses to describe his/her own activities.

We have focused this paper on developing a model for meaning representation rather than in how to express this meaning with linguistic expressions that should be customized for each specific user. The description presented in this paper provides just a general insight about the main components of the model and how they are interrelated. The next step includes to analyze and to describe in depth the three data structures and the four processes.

This paper can be useful to researchers by providing them with a first idea about how to organize the meaning representation of linguistic descriptions of computational processes of data.

Acknowledgments

This work has been funded by TIN2014-56633-C3-1-R and TIN2014-56633-C3-3-R projects from the Spanish "Ministerio de Economía y Competitividad". Financial support from the Xunta de Galicia (Centro singular de investigación de Galicia accreditation 2016-2019) and the European Union (European Regional Development Fund - ERDF), is gratefully acknowledged.

References

J. M. Alonso, A. Ramos-Soto, E. , and K. van Deemter. 2017. An exploratory study on the benefits of using natural language for explaining fuzzy rule-based systems. In *IEEE International Conference on Fuzzy Systems (FUZZ-IEEE)*, pages 1–6, Naples, Italy.

P. L. Berger and T. Luckmann. 2011. *The Social Construction of Reality: A Treatise in the Sociology of Knowledge*. Open Road Media.

P. Conde-Clemente, Jose M. Alonso, E.O. Nunes, A. Sanchez, and G. Trivino. 2017. New types of computational perceptions: Linguistic descriptions in deforestation analysis. *Expert Systems With Applications*, 85:46–60.

A. R. Damasio. 2003. *Looking for Spinoza: Joy, Sorrow, and the Feeling Brain*. Harvest books. A Harvest Book.

A. R. Damasio. 2010. *Self comes to mind. Constructing the conscious brain*. Pantheon books.

H. Gardner. 1987. *The Mind's New Science: A History of the Cognitive Revolution*. Psychology: History. BasicBooks.

D. Gunning. 2016. Explainable Artificial Intelligence (XAI). Technical report, Defense Advanced Research Projects Agency (DARPA), Arlington, USA. DARPA-BAA-16-53.

M. A. K. Halliday and M. I. M. Matthiessen. 1999. *Construing Experience through Meaning: A Language-based Approach to Cognition*. Continuum; Study ed edition (June 3, 2006).

K. R. Popper and J. C. Eccles. 1977. *The Self and Its Brain*. Springer-Verlag, Berlin.

A. Ramos-Soto, A. Bugarín, and S. Barro. 2016. On the role of linguistic descriptions of data in the building of natural language generation systems. *Fuzzy Sets and Systems*, 285:31–51.

E. Reiter and R. Dale. 2000. *Building natural language generation systems*, volume 33. MIT Press.

M. Tomasello. 1999. *The cultural origins of human cognition*. Harvard, New York.

G. Trivino and M. Sugeno. 2013. Towards linguistic descriptions of phenomena. *International Journal of Approximate Reasoning*, 54(1):22–34.

G. Trivino, L. Mengual, and A. Van der Heide. 2009. Towards an architecture for semiautonomous robot telecontrol systems. *Information Sciences*, 179(23):3973–3984.

D. Walton, C. Reed, and F. Macagno. 2008. *Argumentation Schemes*. Cambridge University Press.

Authors Index

Alonso, Jose M., 16

Baum, Kevin, 1

Duan, Manjuan, 6

Horacek, Helmut, 11

Köhl, Maximilian A., 1
King, David L., 6

Schmidt, Eva, 1

Trivino, Gracian, 16

White, Michael, 6

Association for Computational Linguistics
209 N. Eighth Street
Stroudsburg, Pennsylvania 18360

ISBN 978-1-5108-4859-7

CURRAN ASSOCIATES INC.
proceedings.com